POETRY
THAT
MATTERS

JOHN BURCIAGA

Copyright © 2025 by John Burciaga

All rights reserved.
Printed in the United States of America.

ISBN: 979-8-9925945-5-3 (paperback)

Cover image: Dumpfes Rot, No.400 by Wassily Kandinsky, 1927

Published by Winter Island Press
3 Winter Island Road
Salem, Massachusetts 01970

winterislandpress.com

Poetry That Matters

John Burciaga

WINTER ISLAND PRESS

Poetry That Matters

To Linda Lu Burciaga
whose love changed my life

INTRODUCTION

Readers may forgive me for the cheeky title to these poems. I consider myself no better than any other poet. But these are not romantic times, and I want my words to reflect that urgency for those who feel the same.

It may be too much to say that poetry is the most democratic of the arts, for in the hands of the courageous and rebellious poems can all speak truth to power or add insight to critical times. Having said that, one may feel, halfway in, that these are not prophetic words, but I beg you to look closely. All poets are behooved to speak of the obligatory themes of love, nature, family and friends, but not all broach nation, war, justice, science and ancient wisdom that does not mislead but gives us sharp discernment into the human condition.

Some of these poems are hoped to address common themes with a freshness of statement. Others are more serious declarations of what we overlook in our treatment of the weak, vulnerable or powerless; and what we hold true about life, death, human destiny and the world—to move beyond myths and superstitions that deny us a knowledge of reality that would free us from bondage of mind and spirit. The Laws of Thermodynamics, e.g., are of crucial importance—without burden of formulae and computations.

As for love, much is often said poetically but impersonally. I assert it should be personal as to whom we love, and how and why. Nature, family and friends bring us nurture and inspiration--and sometimes unhappiness and hurt. Poetry need not be merely pretty words, but a stretching and empowering of the mind.

Join me in this journey: may we feel a kinship and a mutual blessing throughout. These verses are not perfect and not intended to bring agreement but to cause others to think about what we are all thinking, doing and believing about this human adventure that is not solely sweet or solely bitter, but surely bittersweet and deserving of our greatest powers of reflection.

CONTENTS

Introduction   vii

NATURE

Divinities of the Coming Spring   3
Dirt of Redemption 1: *A Poem of Gratitude*   4
The Seasons   6
Two on Clouds 1   8
Two on Clouds 2   9
Dirt of Redemption 2   10

SCIENCE

Fire and Ice and Asteroids   15
The First Law: *Conservation of Matter*   17
The Second Law: *Entropy, the Invisible Force*   19

ART

In Plein Sight   23
Out of This World: *Into the Abstract*   25
Paper Trail   27
Port of Call   29
Damn Them That Damned Her   31
Everyone a Poet   33
Where Is a Poem?   35

Classical

Her Way   39

Don't Look Back: *The Tragedy of Orpheus and Euridice*   40

Spider Woman: *Myth of Arachne*   42

Marriage of Hector and Andromache   44

Did Sappho Say It?   45

Betrayed by Love: *Dido and Aeneas*   46

Justice

Ashes on the Moon
Native Tribe Opposes NASA Memorial Remains   51

BANG! BANG! We're Dead: *A Performance Poem*   54

Jesus Went to School Today   56

Modern Madonna: *Mamie Till-Mobley Emmet Till 1941-1955*   59

Twenty-Nine Hundred: *Commemorating 9/11/01*   62

Cold Fire and Fiery Cold   65

Ekphrastic

I, Hamlet   69

Mayflower Mother   71

Mona   73

Love

    Portrait of a Lady   77

    Spring Life   78

    Lost Friend   79

    Love and Roses   80

    Love in Winter: *(Cf. Shakespeare Sonnet XCVII)*   82

    In December   83

Aging and Death

    Phone Me   87

    Forgive Me   88

    Life, Death and Time   90

    Death Be Proud   91

    When I Die   92

Acknowledgements   93

NATURE

DIVINITIES OF THE COMING SPRING

If there be gods
They must be wildflowers

DIRT OF REDEMPTION 1
A Poem of Gratitude

I came upon a garden of delights
By true confession
A garden of quiet miracles
Practicing resurrection

Where the ordinary are special creations;
I drink tea of warming mint
Among neighbors of garlic-scape

We who look upward
For inspiration
Must here look down:
Things abundant about our feet
Await our eyes and appetites

May we too be so generous
As to grow in ways
That nourish others;
Here plant our feet
In soil that grows us,
Become a miracle of service
That they may eat our lives
And its poetry
And become their
Delirious existence

Pray that we may be
A garden of delightful miracles
Our bodies holy dirt

THE SEASONS

1

Winter falls, with coat and freeze
of snow,
Icy tentacles of cold;
As if in grip of death
A tomb of ever-ness.
How can anything
So fixed in iron grasp
Be other than forever?

2

Then the Sun from its beyond
Leans in with gift of warm,
Earth unbinds, struggles free
From what was death
To a miracle of amaze:
The fatal grasp on Persephone
Loosens the skin of our spinning world
And bleeds with life unexpected

3

Yet brief is the garden green
As Spring's light mood
Comes to an exalted blaze,
A new and more warm embrace
Free of Janus' hibernal

To new-found Earth
In flourish of balmy breath
And sunlit bake
By alternating turns

4
Then leaves' ripened tones
Come to crisp of colors in startling variation,
Our globe gleams to gold in finest aspects,
Breezes relocate their habitation
Into air and earthly scatter

And to the cautious eye a further hint:
This too is an interim of life,
Impermanence of being,
No eternal succession of imagined stages
But a repetition of known replacement;
No series of surprise
But a wealth of recognition
That all is not everlasting.
Our home alone remains eternal
In its regular revolutions.

TWO ON CLOUDS 1

O what clouds are passing by
Known since world began
Timeless though afloat or still

A panoramic view is theirs
We the lowly ones
With earthbound cares
And mournful tears
Mingle with their airy drops
Ere they depart

Below the roof
Of heaven's blue
We wait return of friendly billows
To shelter our grief
With canopy of quiet
Healing grace

TWO ON CLOUDS 2

Those haughty clouds!
Towered above our earthen state
They come and go as wish.

Forms and faces
In slow but ever-changing
Shapes,
Ghosts they are,
Spectral beings,
Breaking promises as images
For eternal posterity

Being not forever,
They look down
In alternating amity and aloofness,
A snobbery of slight awareness
Of who and what we are

They may as well be aliens
In their worldly disinterest,
We may deem them to be gods
But just as we accept their royalty
and bow in deep genuflection—

                They are gone

DIRT OF REDEMPTION 2

This bath of cleansing rain
Please erase the soil of the former day

Purify my pores
Of poison that is political
And from all that is inimical
To hopes and health

The garden I grew
Rubbed me sore from toil
Meant to bring a joyful harvest
To feed my soul and other souls

But this tarnish won't go away,
I fear it's here another day
And as I look ahead
Is it best to pray
That misery be only mine
And I a savior to my kind?

No, this dirt is hard to clean
When men and outcomes are so mean
And it's hard to keep my mind so sane
And hold not neighbor in my disdain

Or I'll become like him another way
And when I'm old and gray
Who will want my ugly disposition
And my captious inquisitions
On them and their undeserving young?

The garden awaits my hands and sweat;
Gardens too know contamination

But tolerate no condemnation,
They wait for loving care to come
In promising silhouette
To take a chance on life or death
The outcome with bated breath;
And like my shower rain,
Life-giving drops bring growth again
And I'll know
It's more than hope and work
That bring a glad refrain
On this hopeful city on a hill

The answer lays not in the soil--
Dirt is faithful and forever;
But power is also in ourselves:

When weathered and wounded,
Take a breath:
The future awaits our immortality

SCIENCE

FIRE AND ICE AND ASTEROIDS

This poem references Robert Frost's "Fire and Ice" but adds the modern existential concern for dangerous asteroids—and is dedicated to those scientists who study, identify and have proposed methods of deflection of such incoming threats.

If our world becomes a tragic mess
from divine mishap or devil's jest,
by devastation of ice or fire,
it means we're equally doomed entire

So what then--and what the point?--
that all this order gets out of joint
and burns or freezes, as said the poet;
--another twist is added to it:

A heavenly rock, a thing less thought of:
not the kind you'd stub your toe on
or assail glass houses with such a stone;
no, a giant boulder from the sky above

Sisyphus rolled one up a hill:
it rolled back down to his dismay
and at his post was doomed to stay
and repeat his sentence every day until--

--but then there was poor Prometheus
impaled upon a cliff of stone;

his sin, it's said, that he was impious:
giving fire to mortals for our very own

--and made us impious in our own due turn.
So there's fire again--but where's the ice?
Dante said that Hell was more than burn,
that worst of sinners lay in coldest vice

But these are fables now outworn;
from familiar lore we're rudely torn
--back to where there is *that Stone*...
and we're left to tremble all alone.

But *Science* comes to the rescue now
to nudge the meteorite from our brow
and save the day from calamitous row
perhaps to self-destruct, someday, somehow.

THE FIRST LAW
Conservation of Matter

It's said we all were there
at the Fall of Rome
and when the West was Won
when Socrates and Sappho took a breath;
that particles of we and all
intermingled in the thrall
of Valhalla's great and wondrous hall
and it's said: we had a ball

It's said that nothing ever dies,
not saints or sinners, even pesky flies;
we're here and there and everywhere
in times and climes with startled stare,
in times our atoms were ever spared;
We know because, in First Law's eyes
Nothing ever, ever dies

So we're immortal in a way
though over corpses we weep and pray,
but nothing dies, it just goes on
in cycles of recurring dawn

We can thank our stars, however came they,
That nothing can be made or done away with
--as often told from lab and myth—
but a cycle of perpetual energy
from a magical miracle burst of synergy;

and regardless, whether whales or warts, all
is greater than its separate parts

Thanks to science's revealing labors from
dateless days we're best of neighbors and
will be till all this *never* ends—
So I repeat, nor make amends:
Its never over, nor are we—
This goes on for eternity.

THE SECOND LAW
Entropy: the Invisible Force

My morning brew goes hot to cold
I'd rather it were cold to hot
The world withal is much too bold
And contrary than ever thought

My cup would best be thermal in nature
A lasting effect for fondness and taste
Not harshness of yon faraway glacier
But a law best obeyed in this time and place

We're in a world obligated to *work*
There's stubborn disorder, random-like, cruel
That pulls at our neatness with obstinate jerk
Reshuffling structure with continuous pull;

Not predictable as might be preferred
Not even these words arranged into rhyme;
Best intentions are thereby deferred,
For *entropy*, sadly, increases with time

I'll pour my next coffee with this novel thought:
If I'd have it stay warm for comfort and taste,
A new source of energy needs to be brought
To liven my brew—in a manner of haste.

Things stay not the same (and not of our doing);
To Whoever/Whatever made this creation

Contrary to what we're busy pursuing
We should offer no less than best of *reaction*

Let us therefore with accord that is certain
Proceed with knowledge of this obvious quirk:
Effort and knowledge will lift the dark curtain
Or, as Second Law states, nothing will work.

The *Arrow of Time* goes one sole direction
Whatever won't follow is met with assault,
Is brief, artificial and leads to destruction
Regardless unplanned or admitted of fault.

Things go one way or another, that is,
Forward or back, yet never the same
Meaning we must strive for perfection, as is,
Or there's hell to pay in this chaotic game.

ART

IN PLEIN SIGHT

Some creators know no bounds:
In artistic revolt they take to streets,
Parks, fields and farmlands,
Shores of lake and river and ocean-side;
Peer the sky of its many moods
And its billows free;
Truths unknown to frantic eyes
Daunted by mortal distractions

These painters unknown to walls,
Renegades from studio and shelter
Belong to the *immediate*:
They gaze in boldness at what God
And Nature wrought,
Drawing it near that we may benefit
From their wanderings and wonderment
As denizens *en plein air*

These defectors from confinement
Have kin of lofty honor, rarest of inventive DNA:
Monet, master of the illusion of light;
Renoir's rainbow palette of people at play;
Sisley's bridges of the Seine;
These and others, all indentured
To the self-same gift.

Such unchained artists occupy all outdoors,
Their quiet presence commanding curiosity,
Attention and admiration;

We wonder who and what they are
But they, unmoved, are lost
In mysteries of moons and meadows
But always, always in *plein*-est sight

OUT OF THIS WORLD
Into the Abstract

Take a moment's while to see
Language without words:
Line, form, shape and color
Here but not of this world

Masters of the regal Renaissance
Showed the world as we saw it
Though an illusion of reality
Till time and circumstance
Re-shaped it all, and us.

To our wondering eyes
Art held a mirror to what we, unaware,
Had become amid hate, war
And the perils of progress

Artists are where rebels are found,
Embracing freedom elsewhere lost
And revealing another world:
Abstract is its name,
Famous for a world unimaginable

There were Whistler and Matisse;
Munch, Cezanne and their unsettling sights
Cubism and its oddities
Surrealism's flights of fancy;
Mondrian's geometrics of cones, cubes and spheres;

Ghostly features in circles, squares and triangles
A breakdown of all that was familiar

Minimalism and a riot of sensuous color abound;
Bold use of paint to shock and distract,
Distortion reigns in a blaze of brightness,
Objects emotionally charged,
Deranged mental states of being.

Abstraction reflects the way we are,
Our dreams and deliriums,
A re-shaping of reality,
A world *in the abstract*

Yet there is beauty too: lively, lovely imagination Can you tell the difference?

In this moment's while,
Pause and ponder:
You know what you're thinking—
But what are you seeing?

PAPER TRAIL

I am Art
Born as lines and circles on shell and bone,
Painted as pigs in ochre;

Papyrus, hide and wood have been
My given canvas
I've adorned cotton, linen and silk,
I am the face of van Gogh on burlap

I probe the human condition,
I am backdrop to dreams of better worlds;
I am monuments carved to save fading memories

Then came the revolution,
The great Paper Chase
Of accessibility, flexibility and new life for me:
In origami and kirigami;
For composing keen edges of cityscapes, and
The twisted curves of nature and geometric shapes

My future forms are drafted on sketch- and drawing-paper
In pencil, ink and charcoal;,
I live in pastels: in the adornment of quilling;
In tissue—colors and patterns and random shapes,
Or in glued newsprint to catch the eye

I am Art
I decorate the world with beauty, truth and goodness

In stone, metal, ceramic, and found objects,
But I am far, far along the paper trail

New revolutions in Art there are
But creations with the progeny of pulpwood
Have been, are yet and ever will be.
Dwell here awhile amid the magic of art and paper

PORT OF CALL

A river runs through it
Where ocean awaits,
A confluence of art and opportunity
A boardwalk of welcome
For neighbors and newcomers
For the traveler and guest
Seeking the fresher air, a landscape
Inhabited by artists with eager brush,
With style and substance,
In rich hues of the spirit

This is a life-seeker's port of call,
A disembarking to old and new,
Where history was made
In calls to liberty and nation,
To hearts of the enslaved,
Where builders of mighty ships
Went to sea; all past and present are
The artist's motif

Here is a canvas for memory
For the hopes of those who believe
In the power of expectation,
Who have wings to spread and fly
Into reveries of craft and skill

This is Newburyport, a gathering of soulmates
To celebrate friendship and talent;
This is *your* Port of Call:

All that is required is to come and stay
A while or forever, brandishing your palette
Of hopes and aspirations, easels to hold images
Of what you will become

This is Newburyport,
Where heart and history call,
Where you leave the vessel of wandering;
Nomad no more, you are Aeneas arrived
At your Rome, Artemis at her mountaintop,
Where the soul of art and splendor
Will accrue to your present
And for posterity

DAMN THEM THAT DAMNED HER

She would have been this day's
Oliver

But they, those men, condemned
Her woman-ness

It was an earlier time
But tell me not it's their excuse

After war, men had voices legion
She gave one to women

And it was deemed her sin
And they threw her out again

Too personal, they said
To Miss Millay
Too *confessional* and that's not our way
No *intellect* they said

A man's world is here to stay
And so they sent her far away
From Poet's club

But her favor stayed
Among her kind
And other men loved
her mind
but hurdles were too many

She sat atop the stairs,
witches' brew beside
Whether she fell or threw down
her riddled self

She was great at fifty-eight
but so much more would have come
and Mary is your resurrection

As we read the one
we'll know you both
and in all the greats to follow

EVERYONE A POET

O god—
everyone's
  a poet
Each and every
armed with magic pen
whereby to startle
world and men
with versification's obfuscation,
lines verbose of shredded prose
words lachrymose
notions fraught and frozen
in the fire and ice
of apocalyptic vise

How ironic
there's nothing now Byronic,
the modern spirit robbed of tonic

Oh, now everyone's a poet—
my god where came this from
that poetry, once neglected,
if not reviled, stepchild of the
Tolstoyan, Shakespearean
is now the karaoke
of all who are in delirium
of fame and fortune
otherwise sought in
realms impossible
to their art and effort

That once was pinnacle of the
Homeric, Aeschylean:
a mount to look on.
We've made morass of
thoughts and images
mish-mashed

Who judges this mess,
this monumental Fall?
What are the grave odds
we've offended all the gods?
Words pasted all over
surfaces of despair
slung here and there
with devastation
and pretentious sophistication;
from newspaper words errantly cut
and flung on poetry pages but
in gleeful reverie:
Pin the Tail on the Donkey!

Is this but the Capitalism
of this arm of Art
and its slavish consumerism?

In poesy seek
heart and spirit in earnest
or forever wade
in muck and ferment
of sticky verse
wherein there be no forest
for the trees

WHERE IS A POEM?

If I say there is a poem
inside of me
where is it
and of what is it made?

Of matter it is not manufactured
but of mud and mind and wickedness,
a mystical mansion of mistakes,
a reservoir of restlessness, regret
of all that is undone,
unrealized, unrecognized,
held together by threads
of loving moments
that notwithstanding fail to heal
the sadness from all that's unrequited

Poems of perfection are forged
in the furnace of molten dreams
and errant thoughts
of those most foolish,
felons of the heart
executioners of human hopes

There may be poems
that are loveliest of trees
but not from wickedness
are yet set free.

CLASSICAL

HER WAY

Artemis went her sole and splendid way
From birth
Daughter of a god
For whom privilege awaited

Yet made her own vow
And bound herself by oath
And by her sire:
That she would be virgin first and always
Never take a man
Be her own will and compass
And stride highest elevations
Of wood and majestic hills

Then said to him,
Her mighty god-creator:
Let this be!
He did, and the covenant was sealed

And so called was she:
The Mighty Hunter

And Eros knew to stay away

DON'T LOOK BACK
The Tragedy of Orpheus and Euridice

Eurydice, did you love too much
Fleeing with your lover in haste of peril?
Love at times will bring our ruin
For we hold endearment much to heart
With no mind for the unsafe step
Or the will to face our fears

In dispatch to safety
You trod the poison head
Of our ancient foe;
And of life and love
Were you made forfeit

Carelessness is fraught with risk
And even joyous pursuit
May steal our breath
And brevity of life
And oft makes youth respond with haste

Your lover too has his debt:
Rushing you from harm
Then to your everlasting death
Though heroic to reclaim you
With music's sweet seduction
That charmed the Dog of Hell
And even Death himself--

You, Orpheus, gained the path to life
And in your self-same hurry
Saw the light of refuge
But in violation of a sole restriction
Looked too soon
On your lover's yet shadowed face

Dear doomed Pair,
Love does not Conquer All
As we would wish it so;
Youth is fleeting, as is life
And death too soon behind

Though one be near-immortal
Another's poor humanity is best
When firmly safe-secured,
For the lover's bewitching charms
Risk peril to chance and stubborn fate

Step lively but with care
In this vault of happiness and horror
What is precious is not everlasting
And love itself, so ever brief
Makes its pursuit a somber pleasure.

SPIDER WOMAN
Myth of Arachne

Lovely lady, weave your spell
A tapestry of art to tell
A story to enflame the gods
And risk your gift against all odds

Lovely girl, your talent grew
And the wisest goddess quite well knew
You had technique and flair to flout
But wrong to spread it all about

And shun the inspiration quite divine
Thus leaving solely your light to shine
Stealing glory from Athena on high
In your disavowal of humble pie

And the queen of your material gift
Induced a mortal-and-immortal rift,
Reduced your life to death's repose
But not to inactivity, as supposed,

But in a transformation scary
Of form and frame multi-legged, hairy;
Nonetheless with gift intact
To ply your trade for good, in fact,

And forever now we see your work
Where you lie about or lurk

But the moral is never lost in myth
That you live and weave again herewith

That all behold your proven craft
Astonished at your sly witchcraft
But not without the bitter lesson
That talent's not our sole possession

And so we thread our human ways
Through sins and wrongs of normal days
Spinning tales from sites aloof
But ours is not the warp and woof

Of world comprised of smooth rich fabric
Or hard as steel or stone or brick
But the gossamer of our feckless blame
Fashioned on our human loom and frame

MARRIAGE OF HECTOR AND ANDROMACHE

Excitement grew and all the world lost silence
He with bride in tow, she of highest station
And in jewels unnumbered
His sire spread the world in that vast citadel
And Trojans *en masse* made transport
For their many wives who clambered thereon

And all the rest made a world of celebration
Fit for gods and goddesses
With music of every sort, and sacred songs
Prayers too were vastly heard
The universe resounded
And flashed an unknown brilliance
No cost was spared

All this, all this, devoted to
The god-man Hector
And blessed Andromache

O Troy! Thy future awaits

DID SAPPHO SAY IT?

Did Sappho say it?
I don't know
It is worldly wise
And heavenly too
I want it to be true:

"If death be good,
Why do gods not die?
If life be ill,
Why do gods still live?
If love be all,
What should any do but love?"

Dear gods above tell me
Sappho said it so. If not,
Who said it,
Said it well

It is truth to me:
What are gods without life?
What is life without my life?

BETRAYED BY LOVE
Dido and Aeneas

Much is made of woman's lot
And Dido's most grievous;
Shrewd to know that ocean cliffs
Could be her Carthage,
A city famed, and she to make it so.

Her beauty matched by strongest will
Portended boundless power
Enduring fame,
While she, pursued by competing lovers,
One unfit,
One of late ashore from fated Troy

Who but knows her future best
Could have been a sole success
Or, in time, love dearer than Aeneas?

Was it Cupid's Arrow
Or that of Chance
That brought her low
From highest loft?

Love holds opportunity but makes
Minds delirious to know
Which the better way in life or love

Aeneas too was not his own—
Fate cast lot on him as well:
Rome was not, but was to be,
And he as creator chosen

She loved—and lost;
He sailed away to endless honor
And she, to escape the worst of love
Built the fire that would consume her

Yes, well known is she,
Aeneas even better
And Rome best of all
And for eternity

Common lives are quick forgot;
Larger, fairer ones as well, in time;
But all consumed at last by Fate
Or by the Fire that either kills
Or tempers life to best of steel—
Yet it was his blade she thrust into her side
Then fell on the pre-appointed pyre

We pause to say:
Why she the chosen casualty
Save to say she was in a world
That to men belonged
Who most would benefit
From honors claimed

Love is long and eager studied
But at last unknown
Save its result for good or ill:
We stay and prosper
Or live at last to suffer
Or we sail away to build our Rome

But tied we are to our ironic past
And neither is forgotten.

JUSTICE

ASHES ON THE MOON
Native Tribe Opposes NASA Memorial Remains

In rush to claim future's prize
We take shreds
Of our humanity, once living,
To declare we were
Where most do not go

We mark our common place
With earthly remains of life gone by,
Testament to the past
That blessed our soil
With deeds that made us proud

But days to come
Beckon forethought
Of events awaiting;
A new pre-history of times unseen

But what stake to plant on
Distant soil,
Besides emblematic feet
Of astronauts
In foreboding gesture
That more of our kind
Will flood moons, planets
And space between
With cities in the sky?

Here on earth, our oldest kin,
Outside of newest tech and science,
First stewards of our storied soil,
Have other uses for our moon,
Ordained with ancient meanings

Such takes the vastest vision,
Whose dreams inhabit such far place
With hearts, minds
And imagination;
Meanings to claim
That to keep them requires
A challenge to our modern age,
Their plaints but voices
In the wilderness
--A stubborn honor to those of theirs
Who went before, gathering spirits
Of distant but undying past

We and they seek oneness
But there is yet a rift:
The sacred is their past;
For us, the future is the holy

What matter that the dust
Of former life
Makes the longest journey
To a place subordinate to here?

What matters it that human dust
No longer breathing
Finds final refuge in the faraway?

Or what to us, the moderns,
That we insist to say
We own the universe
With every weightless step we take?

Must ashes be the latest war
Of otherness?
Would early strife and slaughter of buffalo
Be fitting as ashes of the moon interred?

If the Moon be a new battlefield,
What remains?

Are their ashes ours to take?
No.
Not even to the moon.

BANG! BANG! We're Dead
A Performance Poem

Another day, another crisis
another sacrifice of children
for those who lost our way
in the dark of uncivil war

To be or not.
To be or not to be
Is *not* the question
Not to be is now
the inevitable command

Where are our children?
BANG! BANG!
They're dead.

Where are we—
nurturers and protectors
mothers and fathers?
Where are our hearts
and minds?
--lost in our violent amusements
where tools of our destruction
are props of our favorite fictions.
BANG! BANG! We're dead.

Where are *you* in the mix
of your freedom and power

to find love, birth young
and make friends?

BANG! BANG! you're dead
to what sustains life most precious
and love too
For your anger is dead,
all that is alive is soon
your regret
BANG! BANG!

Who am *I*--?
I see and declare--
I would wake everyone
but my fear and slumber too are strong
and cannot stir others
from their bewitchment

I own no guns, but
BANG! BANG!
I'm dead.

JESUS WENT TO SCHOOL TODAY

Jesus went to school today
Knapsack on his little back
When one unrestrained that day
Prowled the halls for armed attack
Though eye of guard and doors shut hard
Could not forbid a day so marred
Little Jesus saw all he came to save
Ravaged ere his own lesh died.

The day's report marked deep regret
His unspoiled life could not escape
Such unsuspected harm

Jesus went to university today
Not very far away
The gruesome news had reached his ears;
The lesson of the day was that
Much was to be feared,
Whether classmate, mentor, friend
For mankind sinned through infinity
And fallen short of desired divinity

As Jesus kept detailed note
On laptop of collected learning
Missiles of destruction rang
Before the bell could ring:
His dark and handsome visage
Vanished from adoration's view,

His promised future sorely bared
While halls ran red

*The investigation bore a pleading tone
Of a day of double tragedy*

A man named Jesus went to work
And by aggrieved coincidence
His doom was saddest consequence:
He became a marksman's mark

*The inspector's morbid probe made note
Of a "trinity of tragedy" quote, unquote*

Gray-haired Jesus spent last earthly days
In retirement's place of caring ways;
Time passed in mind of labors done
Then he and all met with brutal gun;
A crazed, unwelcome guest intruded
With mortal issues of his own dispute

A passing priest fetched from the ground
A blood-stained backpack and intoned
That Father, Son and Holy Ghost
Suffered death that day;
That earthly hope was surely lost,
For in these hapless murders
Each and all the world had lost
The one they loved the most

We'll still send thoughts and prayers above
But only stop this madness when
It's one we really love

MODERN MADONNA
Mamie Till-Mobley   Emmet Till 1941-1955

Mamie, like Mary,
Chosen to bear
A child of hope
And lose him
To Inhumanity

In this world
Between your grief and Hers
Is nothing to be learned
But that this would happen again?

Holy Mary, as a youth,
Holds her son, fully grown
Upon her everlasting lap
Her dear and helpless child
Vulnerable to wicked men

Yours, Mamie,
So young to be so far from home
And from mother's love
When man-monsters
Savaged him alive
And savaged him in death
They, like Herod, fearful of a child

The sculptor laid Mary's child
Upon her arms

But none there were for Emmet
Whose Mother-Madonna cried out
Like Rachel in the wilderness
In her grief
Because her child was no more

Mamie Madonna made us look upon
His face
To see what was done
To his childhood
And his future
And to his suffering Mother

Mary's child lay forever now
Upon the cold marble lap of love
That he can never feel;

Mamie's, lifted from the
Unholy water of
Tortured death
Raised forever on the Cross
Of the violence that killed him

This Mother
This modern Madonna
Her lap as bare
As her womb
And her heart

O Pieta!

Pieta!

Pieta!

Pity!

Pity us

That we cannot
Rid our world
Of this

TWENTY-NINE HUNDRED
Commemorating 9/11/01

Twenty-nine hundred began a day
And by night lay at our feet
Speaking to us
From graves of dust and ash

It helps not to know what happened
Such is neither expected, dreamed of
Or wanted
Such things pass all understanding
They are the unreal become real

We cannot raise the twenty-nine hundred
They lay at our feet
Grim reminders looking up
For there is no farther down
Dead is dead and there is no farther down:
We are here and they are there

So this is hell and we are in it
Things two or more can be
At once and the same time true:
We live in sunshine and in storm
In cool morning air
And in a hail of bullets,
A blitzkrieg of airplanes
Bears people who will be
Bombs and battering rams
Not of their choosing

Who never voted for or volunteered
To be missiles of murder;
They prayed to God and to
Their mobile phones:

Heard, if not by God, by dear ones
Equally unwilling;
All prayed in desperation
All prayed in resignation
They were we, save that we and they
Were in different places.

Things that murder are all the same:
People are bullets,
Bullets are airplanes,
Airplanes are bullets;
Buildings are infernos,
Infernos are buildings

The twenty-nine hundred lay at our feet
Begging for justice
We hover above, ghost-like
Bereft of justice and mercy;
Given to anger, hurt and helplessness
We imagine justice
But justice is a sometime thing

Time, we say, will bring justice
But in a world, a universe away;
We cannot wait
We can hardly wait

But the dead will be always
At our feet
When they are no longer heard
By tides of time and memory
Then the very stones will cry out
And we will cry with them

COLD FIRE AND FIERY COLD

I would not marry heaven to hell
in bond unholy
for in dark and light reality
are Right and Wrong

We're long excused of innocence
and frail naivete;
our way is fraught
with steps our own

Like the first and earthly Pair,
we name the animals that populate
brooding wood and cave
with rough truth and imagination seductive

and are left to save ourselves
as forest fawns have ever done
when stag and doe
met crude obliteration

from their childhood eyes,
and not knowing why
ventured on to life or death

Longer is our human brand
with more talents to survive by
Yet from nemesis of war
that is clearly of our making
we suffer more

The larger conflict
Is of mind and notion fateful;
we arrive at peril by singular steps
yet think that horror comes
by blinding instant
because our eyes,
too large for life's details,
are too small for the larger view

We'll best keep favored focus
on what is truth and error
when the fire seems cold
and the cold seems fiery

EKPHRASTIC

I, HAMLET

I, victim of injustice
And its purveyor too
I, sleepless nights have known
From grievance to me and my kin
And, I, in my self-doubt,
My inaction a sore recollection;
Given as well to skill and courage
But in equal measure
Stunned to serious silence
When revenge surely called for,
Or worse perhaps, my hurting one most loved.

But stakes are sure unequal
Twixt me and the Danish prince
Who was near throne's pedestal
While betrayed by parent well,
But those not faithful in little
Are known not faithful in much
And, I, hoist of my own petard thereby
Admit to folly of my own

And all of us more lowly
Are no less held to standards high,
For life rests on faithful sorts
To each its parts,
A web connected by devoted hearts
In unison protection

So who is Hamlet: our brother only
By humanity?
But who has not lost a sire,
Though not by savage murder,
Or suspected kinfolk of it?

Or lost a mother's love—
A thing also rare
Though we tremble at its thought?
Who has not disappointed self
Or failed to exercise the dare,
Stood dead in vacillation
And allowed the wrong, and worse,
Full frozen by deadly fear?

All heroes and half-wits
In the world's ample cast
Of victors and villains,
Guilty of misdemeanor or murder
Are our constituent parts;
All may surmise which degree they may fill.
But my admission, lest I forget,
Am known to myself if not others as
I, Hamlet

MAYFLOWER MOTHER

The Mayflower,
Our Mother, bearing our forebears
To where we yet abide

Our matron of memory,
What manner of mom was she?
Quite like so many, multi-made
In kind and meaning

To the olden who knew her
She was first and best, namesake to
Happy symbols of joy, truth,
Love and luck
And yes of Motherhood, a fit designation
For one who bore her children
To a new and promising shore

Given as well to month of May
As abiding Flower of nativity;
Blood and birth
Were her beginning too:
From mortal combat of
Saint and Dragon and what coursed
Through both their veins, spilled aground
And from such soil her petals sprang

Thus born in seeds of conflict
She would have the children of her own
Fertile womb go to safety from

All ills and conflicts
To a new birthright of freedom

But more's the truth to what's at last
A varnished tale:
Her perfumed maternity
Requiring shade and moistened soil
Transforms a bell of purest white
To berry of the reddest red,
Atop the greenest stem

This mother of all mothers,
Rumored to be as well
From the tears of Eve as she left in shame
Her perfect primeval home
Maybe savored by eye
But not of tongue
For both petal and berry bring one
Not to death but to its door

And so may some mothers be,
For none is perfect, but truth,
Oft two-sided, will show its head
As flowers flaunt their beauty or deception
Or mix prettiness with poison

Hence this Mayflower by name
May try our understanding
But to its modern call we rally
What now to us is known
As Lily of the Valley

MONA

Mona
May I call you Mona?
I know you well as artists tell
Of your glory in the story
Of you and your creator

The fame of your enigmatic smile
That long went out of style
From your world of thoughts elusive
To ours of mood effusive.
You were a beauty, it is said
In your day and time
And while other beauty fled
Yours haunts this modern rhyme

Or is it a smile?—
Or mild bemusement
At thought or thing you were observing?
Did your author seek to temper joy
And liven your dismay
At your husband's puckish early day,
Or a lover's fresh abandon?
No, there's a sentiment most pleasant
In what was past, now present
And you may have stubbornly resisted
The artist's petulant insistence
That you flirt with his advances,
And agree to take your chances

That mate or swain might come upon
Your tryst.

Speculation begs another no:
Not a dangerous ego
But impending motherhood,
The expectant other-hood,
Given an embryo lost before
And your instinct wanted more
And that half-smile begs both loss and gain
So that grief and joy in fact are twain
And the so-called smile is both this and that

No again. The future wants you
Starkly virtuous
So the acclaim of all of us
Will hold your simple chastity
To persist into eternity

So forgive that I call you Mona
As if intimate with your persona
You are there for all the world to see;
I only ask that you smile at me

LOVE

PORTRAIT OF A LADY

Poets abound that write of a Lady
Portrait of a Lady, as commonly called

But what or which lady?
Is she a lady?
Must one be a "lady"?

If assumed a woman
we know the attraction
to both women and men

Is she a beauty, brilliant, a sophisticate,
chic and stylish, bosomed and leggy?
Self-possessed, independent, assertive,
self-starting?

Is what she wants in love
sex, dominance, a milquetoast,
blushing maiden, dashing man,
a slave?

What makes a Lady?
What becomes of a Lady:
Feminine, masculine,
bi. non-binary, trans?

Was Sappho a Lady?

Should I want that Lady?
Would she want me?

SPRING LIFE

The ground gives up not easily
Yet Spring it knows is coming

Spring will win its inevitable crown
Of multi-colors, glowing skies
And richest rain

My long winter lay hard
Upon a death of hope and feeling--
First months' stony landscape
Of snow and ice
Where I lay beneath the surface
Of finer things,
A calm death of perceived content

You are my springtime
Clothing me in refreshing
Showers and rainbows
My head rises with the crocus
And waves with nodding daffodils

My cross aside
I rise one day at a time
The winter night is lifted

I live in April
I welcome May

LOST FRIEND

I saw him again
in a dream of course
because he's nowhere else
I could not with him stay
for he kept from me away
in sight, but quite untouchable

It was good to have him even there
I forgot his flaws
and saw his often kindnesses
but he kept away
the livelong day

I lost him then
in the crowd and mist
yet for a time I was surely blest

Where he really is
there is no knowing
Perhaps a nowhere place,
he was here
then he was not;
a long time here,
and there he's ever longer

He was a friend
and still he is
and is again

LOVE AND ROSES

My roses, whose threat is winter
Last unto November
Though flowers hardier
Long since are spent

True, my blossoms grow together,
Though elder blooms lend their heads
To sad remove so others live,
That sun and water grow the new

Yet all endure the loss
That engenders gifts of life
Till at winter's sure behest
All lie down in patient slumber
Till spring arouse from season's rest

Such is my love,
Gift to what we mortals own
The briefest breath
To come as others go
And go as others come

But in the sweetest interim
Is a glow that should never die
But does and will
Yet leaves a thought
That's immortal still;
A thought that will

Keep this heart of mine alive
Despite death's December chill

Why this rare gift is mine I'll never know;
Why earth and time
Bestows this treasure
Till our eyes will someday close
Though this is sure:
The gift was an eternal rose

LOVE IN WINTER
(Cf. Shakespeare Sonnet XCVII)

This winter has assault of harshest wind
The cold not half as bad as were it not
Had I the heartfelt word your way to send
It would be a verse of most fervent thought
I'd warm the chill at fireside of my heart
And use my breath to send it all your way
No frost or gale could keep us far apart
Nor hold my love from you in sad delay
Frigid months require the warmest ever
Of hearts with passion for the weary soul
That no icy breeze would come to sever
Or dare to make our oath a thing to spoil
This great love will last through peace or war
And we'll dwell forever among the stars

IN DECEMBER

Never leave me in December, ever
This everlasting bond to sever
Never leave me when the cold invades
And cuts my icy mood like skating blades
Hold me when wintry winds belay
My spirit and my soul and I betray
A loss of heart as if to say
I seem to you so less a man
In doubt of if I can't or can
Hold you in my heart and mind
Till all the more of love we find.

Never leave me in December, ever
Don't leave me, never leave me, ever

Hold me close in the Solstice-turning
In Hanukkah's age-old candles burning
On Christmas in its blissful cheering
And in the New Year's past a-clearing
Love me in the rage of winter
Its days of quiet snow so gentle
That lay across the mountain's lintel
Clasp my hand when storms do threaten
And avalanche of freezing reckons
To rend our loving bonds asunder
Then hold me dear with loving wonder

Let nothing in the world us sever
Nor leave me in December, ever

AGING and DEATH

PHONE ME

I call, no answer
no recording, no call returned
This wall of silence deafens
and there are things I need to know:
Are you ok? Are you coming back?
How are those we knew?
I'm full of news I want to share
and you were great at listening
and I don't like the sound
of my own voice
echoing back to me

Do I sound far away?
Have I offended, spoken out of turn?

Oh, I get it,
you're not here, you're there

But we'll meet again,
Don't know where
Don't know when

Remember that old song?
There's something to it.
I love you
I love all of you I knew

And I can wait

FORGIVE ME

I ask you to forgive me
In advance

Youth and vigor have been ours
Hope and promise were our towers

Walking in the light did not blind:
Daffodils shone brightest then
Even dandelions in fields they rent
In early Spring, commanding eye
And compliment
Such were the days
That belonged to us

With gift of being full aware
We walked a seemed eternity
Yet future now has credibility:
Given paradise to dwell in
Love has limited infinity

Though ours a gift most generous
We see shadows of forewarn
That compel our heed
And I beg you honor this last request
Regardless of the gracious past
While suspect of what tomorrow bring:

Light is everything and all,
And dark another, sober time
Unlike our rest in arms together

Each and every night's forever
That the morrow bring another light

Darkness may stalk our loving breath
That one of us may--worse than death--
Enter shadows of earnest grasp
And hold us in such grip too fast,
And whisk away in time
To place defiant of plea or rhyme
To where we can't return
Though all else be perceptible

Will you vow,
If in a place I would not be
And fail to know you as I do,
To think of me as in other day?

God forbid I deem another soul
Would be another you
And seem to turn away
And embrace what is not true
Such I'd not allow in best of mind
Please know I'm not there in sort or kind

I'm yours in every way that's true and real
Though a thief ofttimes concealed
An abundant truth would dare to steal

If comes such day and time obverse
Lay your eyes upon this verse,
Hold this though such time seem far
And I'll hold your place among the stars.

LIFE, DEATH and TIME

Can I die now?
I'm not the kind
Time's a factor here
and though I'm always
quite on time
exactly what's the time
to live or die?

Living-time has much to do
with early, late or
right on time.
Death has only one
and always on its time

So *time's* the thing here
and though I'm always
quite on time,
I must say that
regarding death
I'm not the kind,
and I *really* haven't
got the time

DEATH BE PROUD

Death be proud
there are so many ways,
mortal being but the least:

Ruin of memory, pain, regret;
death of mind, unrighteous rival
where flesh remains but all else lost,
rued most of all by those who love them so

Death as well
in soulless disregard
for others' grief
or disadvantage of time and birth
or on whom despair of disease
lays grave assault;
and death of generosity
that makes all gain ill begot,
and those who slay their
many thousands
in tyrannies old and new

There is death all 'round
this breathing earth:
it claims all who will be born

So death be proud,
to be many in your
Oneness
We wear your pride unto the death
that is our own

WHEN I DIE

When I die
I will die
not in substance
but in form

All of me, like thee, be history
of something made of something else
and another something I will be

I'd not be planted near yonder tree if I
could I'd be in air
as far as eye could see

But such requires a burn by fire
in noxious ruin of chemical
lest I owned a pyre
that to toxin is polemical

If I lay beneath the tree
earth will claim what's left of me and
I'll break down in all my articles to
other matter's clutch of particles and
be with all that's ready-grown

So then lay me by the tree
but say not I am there
For I am every thing
and I am everywhere

ACKNOWLEDGEMENTS

The poet Tennyson said, "I am a part of all that I have met," and I bring many years of living and several careers and occupations to my poetry.

The greatest influences on me were those who have loved me, at times more than I deserved. The Dedication to this book is for the one who came to me at a crucial time and transformed my inspirations and aspirations: Linda Lu Burciaga opened my eyes and my heart to greater possibilities and given me my happiest and most fulfilling years.

My sister, Mary Lee, who taught me to walk, was the one in my immediate family that most believed in me regardless of my early difficulties, failures and shortcomings.

Rev. Dr. James Gary Blaine may not realize how much his friendship, ministry, colleagueship and remarkable written meditations have helped me see beyond myself.

Thanks to Maile Black and Winter Island Press, who saw value enough in these words to trust their publication. She was superb to completion, honoring deadlines and date of print. One could not ask for more.

Others receive my personal thanks in direct ways and for all of them I, like Sebastian in Shakespeare's Twelfth Night, "can no other answer make but thanks, thanks and ever thanks."

Winter Island Press edits, produces, and publishes books that reflect the breadth and bounty of human experience. Our roster of authors represents a vibrant tapestry of voices. We are delighted to work with both seasoned writers and promising debut authors who contribute to the literary mosaic that defines Winter Island Press. We value creativity, originality, and craftsmanship. From fun and potent fiction to thought-provoking nonfiction and poetry, Winter Island Press publications offer narratives that leave a lasting impact on readers' hearts and minds.

www.ingramcontent.com/pod-product-compliance
Lightning Source LLC
Chambersburg PA
CBHW020553030426
42337CB00013B/1077